Teaching Little Fingers to Play
Disney Tunes
Piano Solos with Optional Teacher Accompaniments
Arranged by
Glenda Austin

MW01055375

CONTENTS

Book
ISBN-13: 978-1-4234-3120-6

Book/CD
ISBN-13: 978-1-4234-3123-7

WILLIS MUSIC

EXCLUSIVELY DISTRIBUTED BY

HAL•LEONARD®
CORPORATION
7777 W. BLUEMOUND RD. P.O. BOX 13819 MILWAUKEE, WI 53213

Visit Hal Leonard Online at
www.halleonard.com

Hint!—
Notice the ties on the last beat of many measures.
Be sure to clap and count out loud.

Student Position
One octave higher when performing as a duet

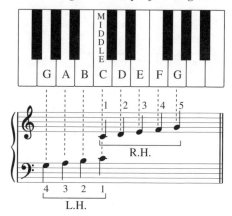

G A B C D E F G

1 2 3 4 5
R.H.

4 3 2 1
L.H.

Can You Feel the Love Tonight
from Walt Disney Pictures' THE LION KING
Optional Teacher Accompaniment

Music by Elton John
Lyrics by Tim Rice
Arr. Glenda Austin

Very gentle and smooth

mp

Can You Feel the Love Tonight

from Walt Disney Pictures' THE LION KING

Music by Elton John
Lyrics by Tim Rice
Arr. Glenda Austin

Play both hands one octave higher when performing as a duet.

Very gentle and smooth

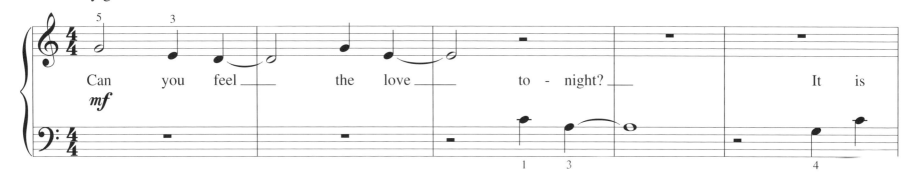

Can you feel ___ the love ___ to - night? ___ It is

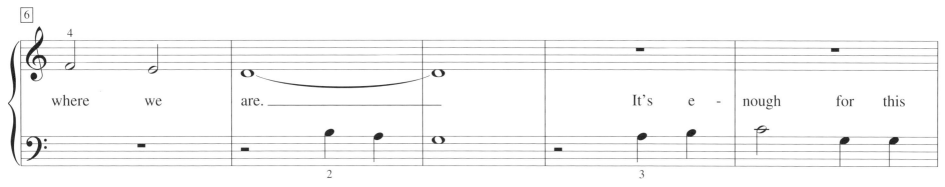

where we are. ___ It's e - nough for this

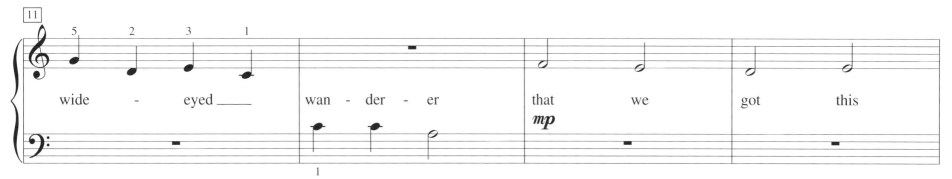

wide - eyed ___ wan - der - er that we got this

Optional Teacher Accompaniment

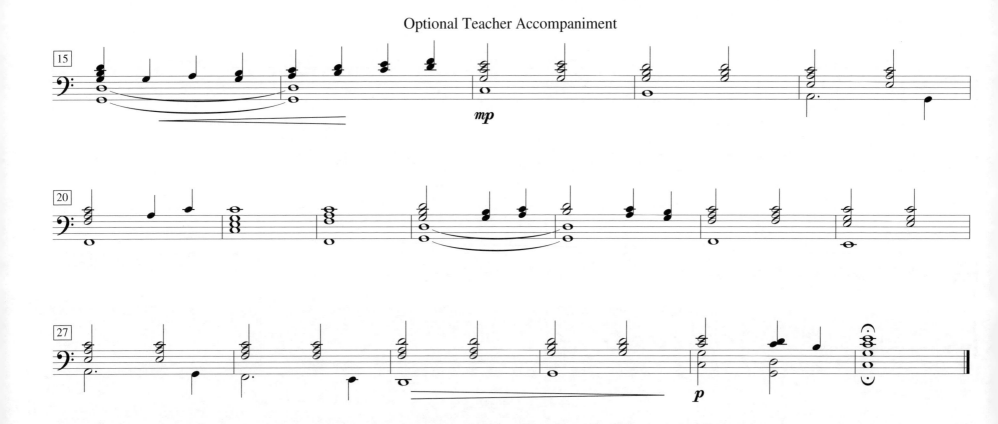

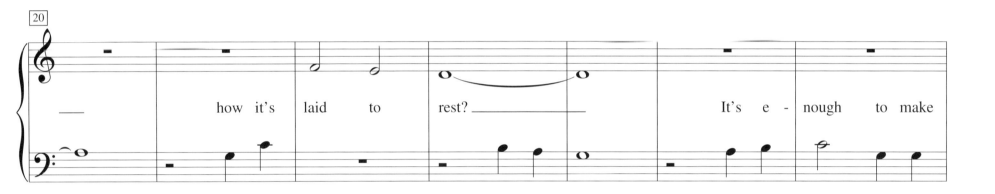

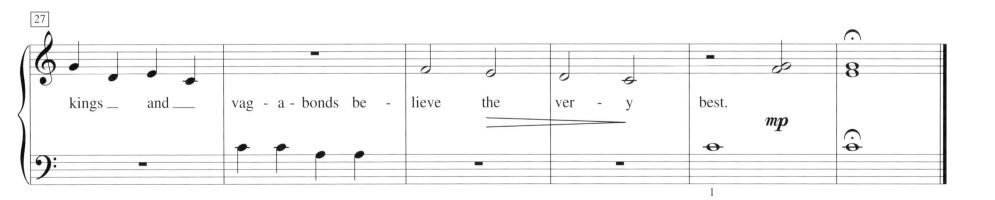

6

Hint!—

Practice drawing a quarter rest: ___ ___ ___
There are many in this piece; most are on
the first beat of each measure.

Student Position

One octave higher when performing as a duet

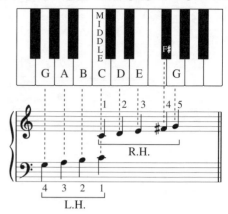

Candle on the Water

from Walt Disney's PETE'S DRAGON
Optional Teacher Accompaniment

Words and Music by Al Kasha
and Joel Hirschhorn
Arr. Glenda Austin

Candle on the Water

from Walt Disney's PETE'S DRAGON

Words and Music by Al Kasha
and Joel Hirschhorn
Arr. Glenda Austin

Play both hands one octave higher when performing as a duet.

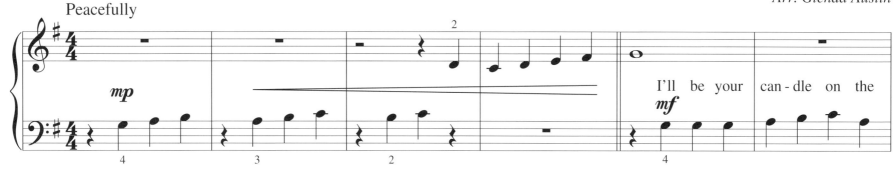

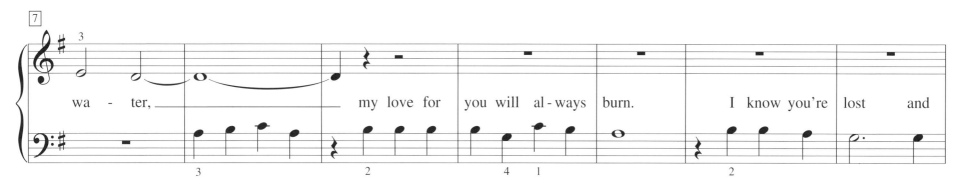

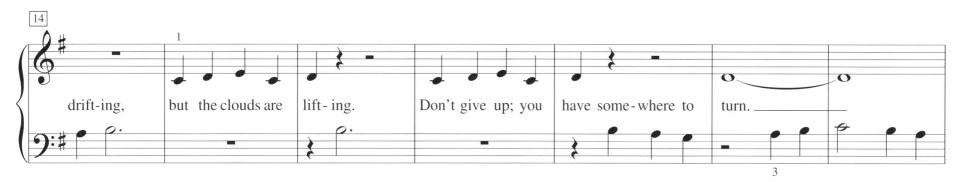

8

Optional Teacher Accompaniment

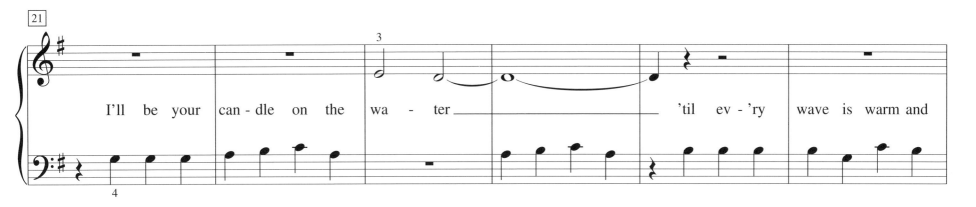

I'll be your can - dle on the wa - ter _____ 'til ev - 'ry wave is warm and

bright. My soul is there be - side you, let this can - dle guide you;

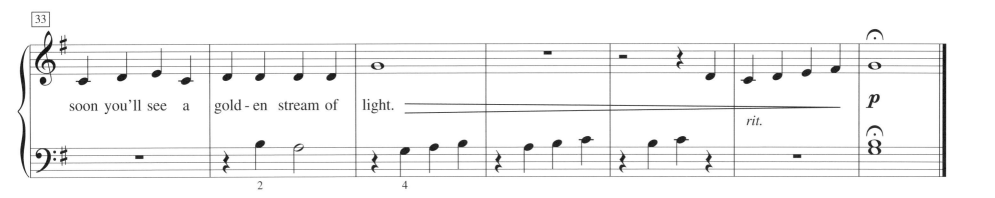

soon you'll see a gold - en stream of light. _____

rit.

p

Hint!—
Be aware that the 5th finger of the L.H. plays F#.

Student Position

One octave higher when performing as a duet

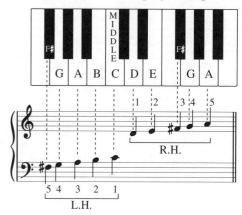

You'll Be in My Heart
(Pop Version)
from Walt Disney Pictures' TARZAN™

Optional Teacher Accompaniment

Words and Music by
Phil Collins
Arr. Glenda Austin

You'll Be in My Heart

(Pop Version)
from Walt Disney Pictures' TARZAN™

Words and Music by
Phil Collins
Arr. Glenda Austin

Play both hands one octave higher when performing as a duet.

Gently

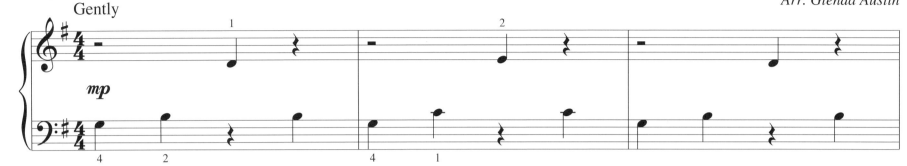

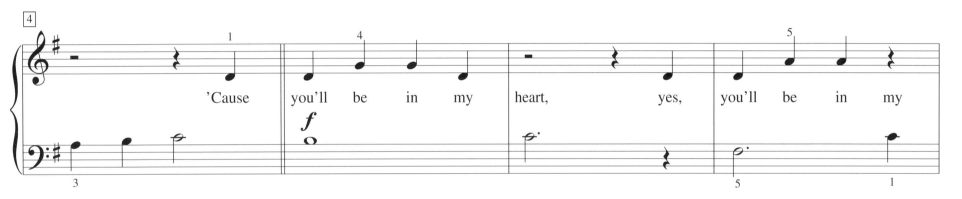

'Cause you'll be in my heart, yes, you'll be in my

heart from this day on now and for - ev - er - more.

12

Optional Teacher Accompaniment

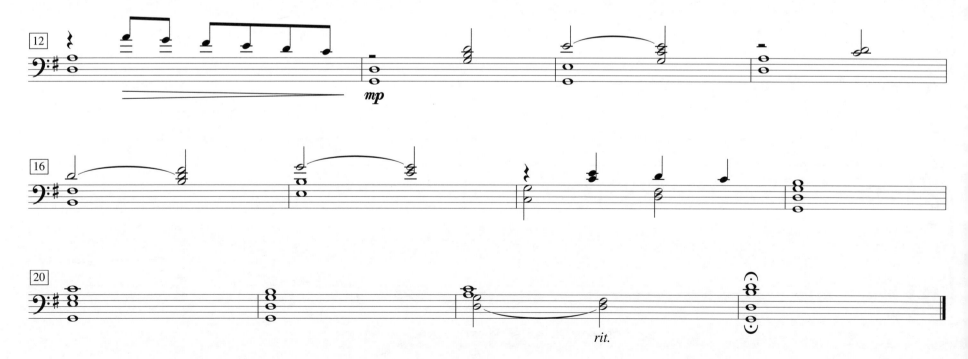

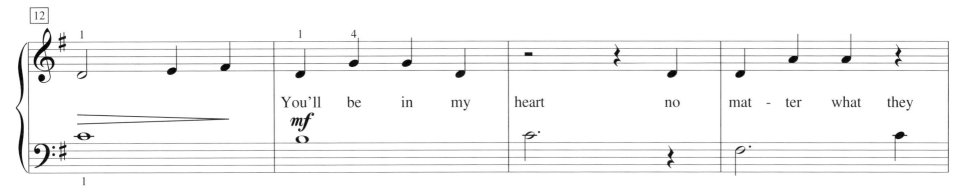

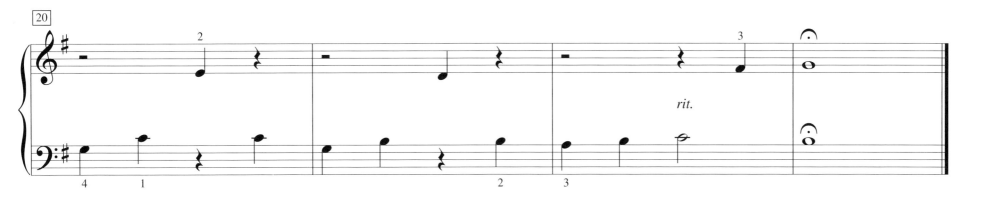

14

Hint!—
Be aware that the 5th finger of the L.H. stretches down to a low D.

Student Position
One octave higher when performing as a duet

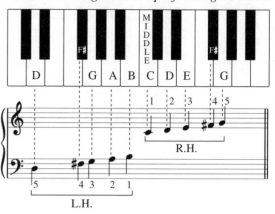

God Help the Outcasts
from Walt Disney's THE HUNCHBACK OF NOTRE DAME

Optional Teacher Accompaniment

Music by Alan Menken
Lyrics by Stephen Schwartz
Arr. Glenda Austin

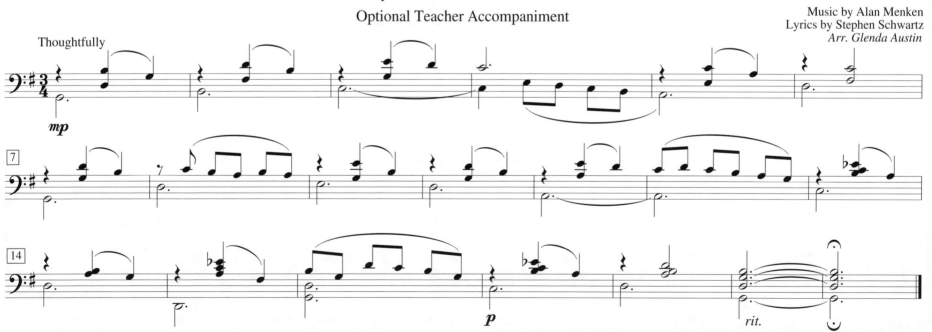

God Help the Outcasts

from Walt Disney's THE HUNCHBACK OF NOTRE DAME

Music by Alan Menken
Lyrics by Stephen Schwartz
Arr. Glenda Austin

Play both hands one octave higher when performing as a duet.

Thoughtfully

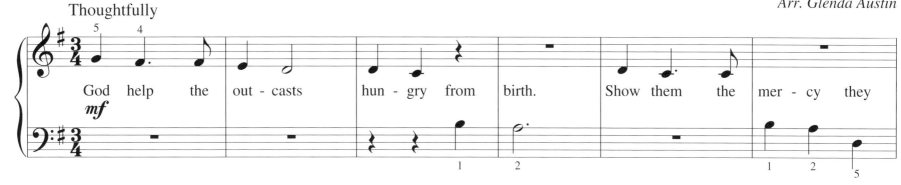

God help the out-casts hun-gry from birth. Show them the mer-cy they

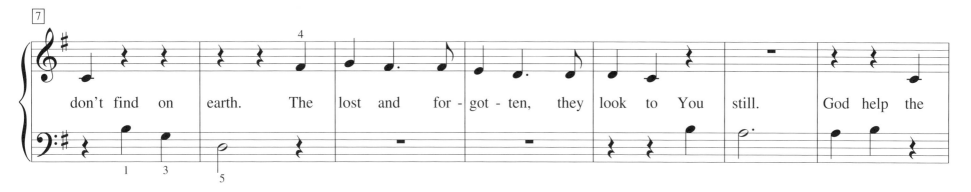

don't find on earth. The lost and for-got-ten, they look to You still. God help the

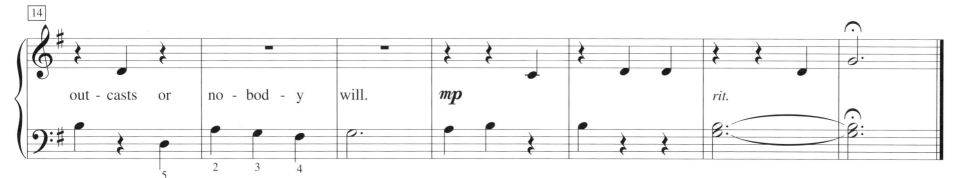

out-casts or no-bod-y will.

Hint!—
Be ready for the L.H. cross-over in measure 10.

Student Position

One octave higher when performing as a duet

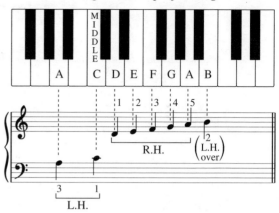

Kiss the Girl
from Walt Disney's THE LITTLE MERMAID

Optional Teacher Accompaniment

Lyrics by Howard Ashman
Music by Alan Menken
Arr. Glenda Austin

Kiss the Girl

from Walt Disney's THE LITTLE MERMAID

Lyrics by Howard Ashman
Music by Alan Menken
Arr. Glenda Austin

Play both hands one octave higher when performing as a duet.

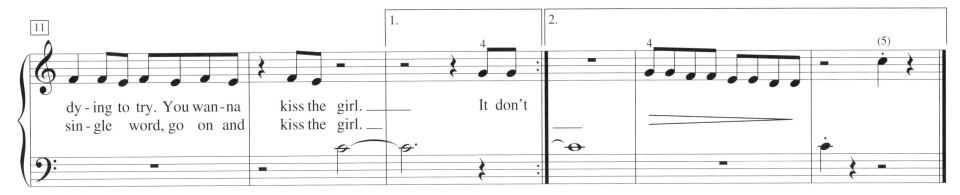

Hint!—
- Notice that the R.H. only has two different note groups to play throughout the entire piece!
- Be ready for the L.H. cross-overs in measures 1, 3, 12 and 13.

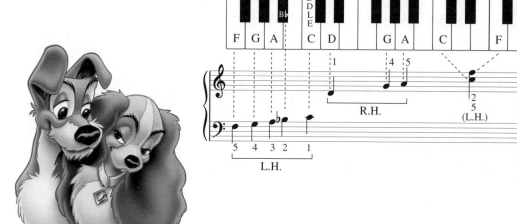

Student Position
One octave higher when performing as a duet

The Siamese Cat Song
from Walt Disney's LADY AND THE TRAMP
Optional Teacher Accompaniment

Words and Music by Peggy Lee
and Sonny Burke
Arr. Glenda Austin

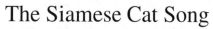

The Siamese Cat Song

from Walt Disney's LADY AND THE TRAMP

Words and Music by Peggy Lee
and Sonny Burke
Arr. Glenda Austin

Play both hands one octave higher when performing as a duet.

Playfully

Hint!—
Pay very close attention to the fingering
in this piece.

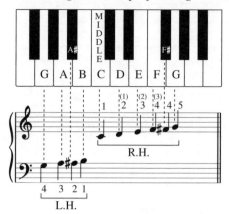

Student Position
One octave higher when performing as a duet

Winnie the Pooh
from Walt Disney's THE MANY ADVENTURES OF WINNIE THE POOH

Optional Teacher Accompaniment

Words and Music by Richard M. Sherman
and Robert B. Sherman
Arr. Glenda Austin

Winnie the Pooh

from Walt Disney's THE MANY ADVENTURES OF WINNIE THE POOH

Words and Music by Richard M. Sherman
and Robert B. Sherman
Arr. Glenda Austin

Play both hands one octave higher when performing as a duet.

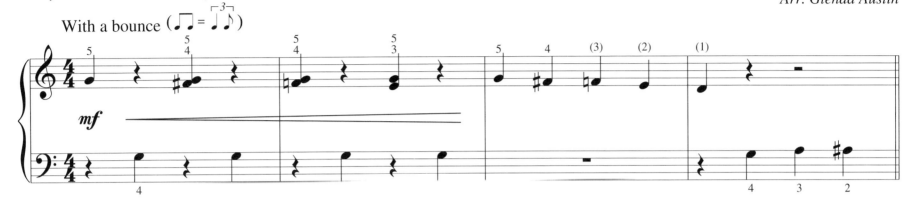

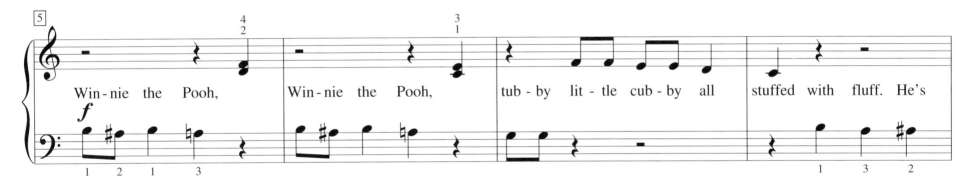

Win - nie the Pooh, Win - nie the Pooh, tub - by lit - tle cub - by all stuffed with fluff. He's

Win - nie the Pooh, Win - nie the Pooh, wil - ly nil - ly sil - ly old bear.

22

Hint!—

Both hands share Middle C! Also pay especially close attention to the L.H. fingering in measures 5 and 6. It repeats many times throughout the piece.

Student Position
One octave higher when performing as a duet

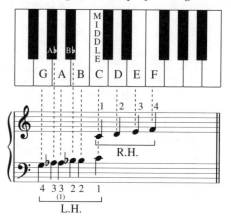

Mickey Mouse March
from Walt Disney's THE MICKEY MOUSE CLUB
Optional Teacher Accompaniment

Words and Music by
Jimmie Dodd
Arr. Glenda Austin

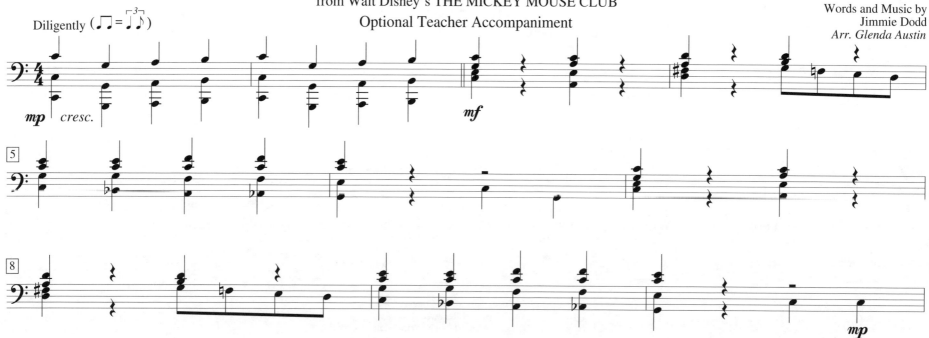

Mickey Mouse March
from Walt Disney's THE MICKEY MOUSE CLUB

Words and Music by
Jimmie Dodd
Arr. Glenda Austin

Play both hands one octave higher when performing as a duet.

Optional Teacher Accompaniment

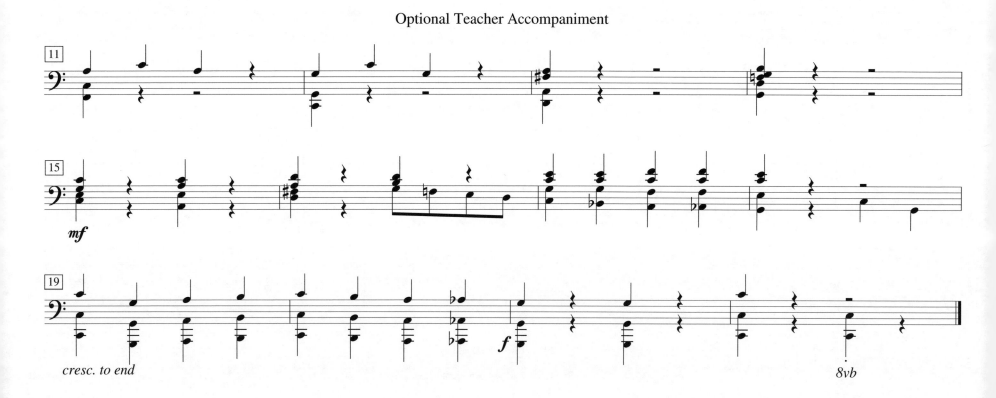

Mouse! Mick-ey Mouse! For - ev - er let us hold our ban - ner high!

Come a - long and sing a song and join the jam-bo - ree! M - I - C - K - E - Y M - O - U - S - E!

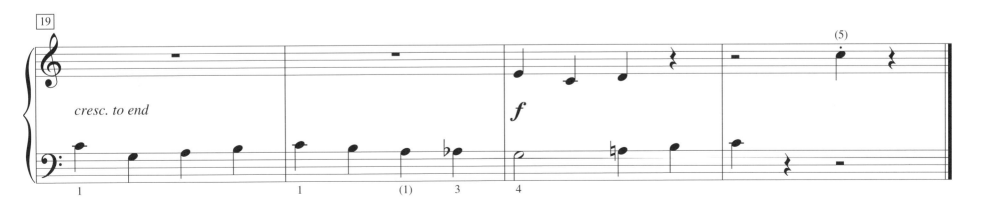

cresc. to end

Hint!—

Like the first tune in this book, notice the ties on the last beat of many measures. Be sure to clap and count out loud.

Student Position

One octave higher when performing as a duet

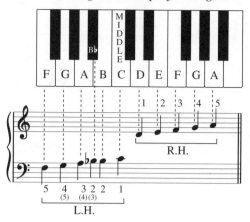

Zip-A-Dee-Doo-Dah

from Walt Disney's SONG OF THE SOUTH

Optional Teacher Accompaniment

Words by Ray Gilbert
Music by Allie Wrubel
Arr. Glenda Austin

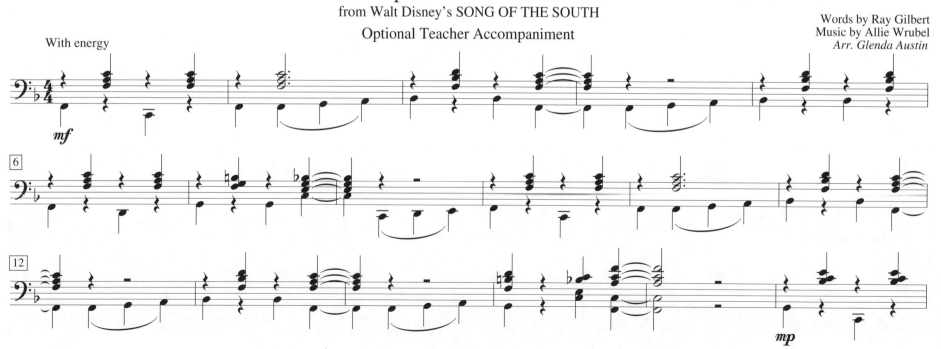

Zip-A-Dee-Doo-Dah

from Walt Disney's SONG OF THE SOUTH

Words by Ray Gilbert
Music by Allie Wrubel
Arr. Glenda Austin

Play both hands one octave higher when performing as a duet.

With energy

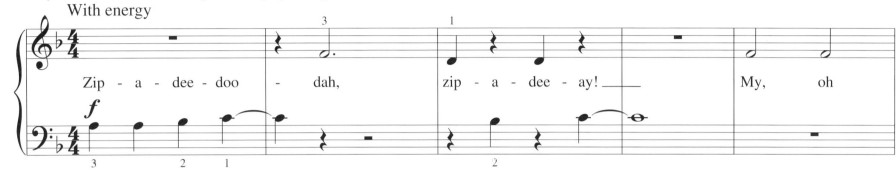

Zip - a - dee - doo - dah, zip - a - dee - ay! My, oh

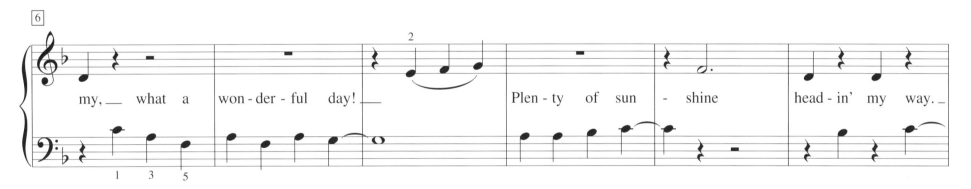

my, __ what a won - der - ful day! Plen - ty of sun - shine head - in' my way. __

Zip - a - dee - doo - dah, zip - a - dee - ay! Mis - ter Blue - bird

Optional Teacher Accompaniment

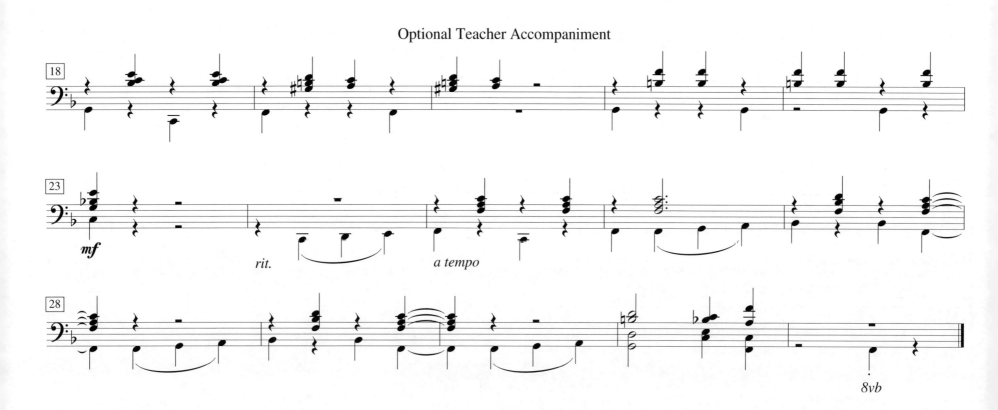

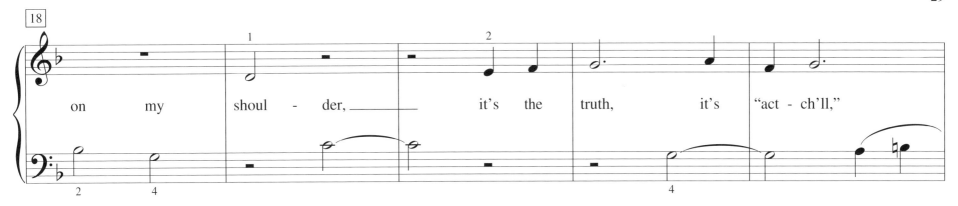

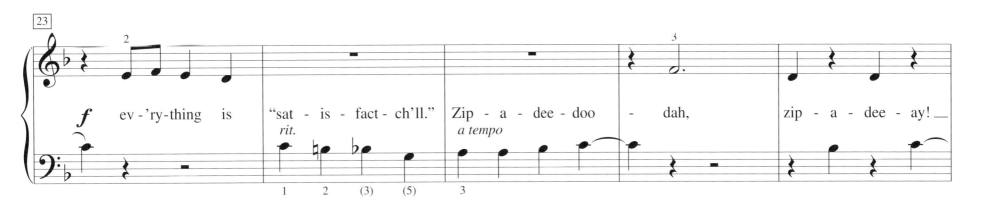

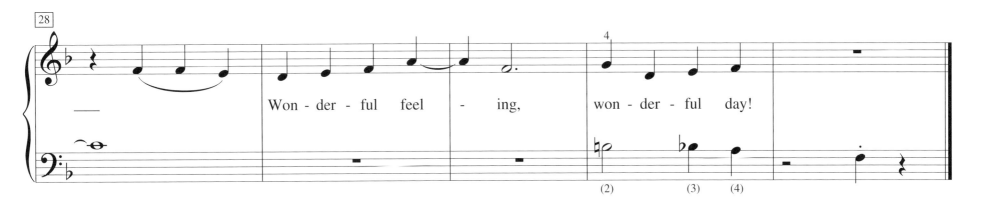

Hint!—
In measure 5, notice that the right hand crosses over the thumb.

Student Position
One octave higher when performing as a duet

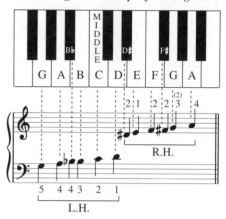

The Bare Necessities
from Walt Disney's THE JUNGLE BOOK
Optional Teacher Accompaniment

Words and Music by
Terry Gilkyson
Arr. Glenda Austin

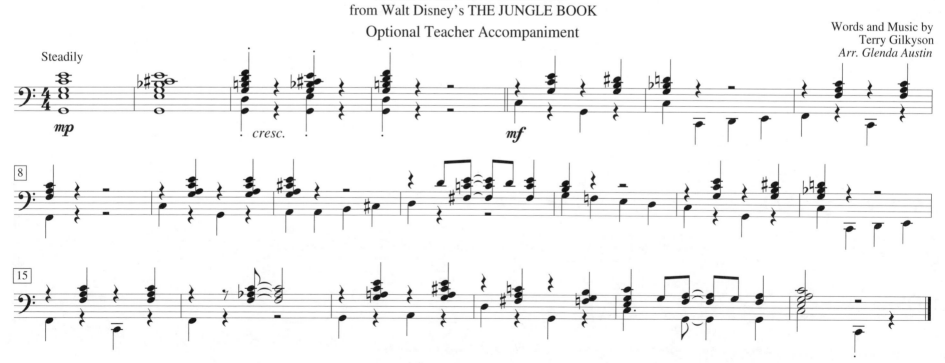

The Bare Necessities

from Walt Disney's THE JUNGLE BOOK

Words and Music by
Terry Gilkyson
Arr. Glenda Austin

Play both hands one octave higher when performing as a duet.

Steadily

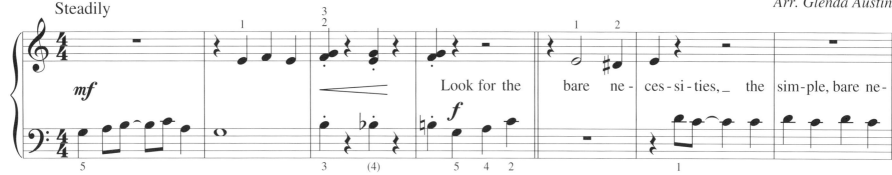

Look for the bare ne - ces - si - ties,_ the sim - ple, bare ne-

ces - si - ties. _ For - get a - bout your wor - ries and your strife. I mean the bare ne - ces - si - ties,_ oh,

Moth - er Na - ture's re - ci - pes _ that bring the bare ne - ces - si - ties_ of life.

TEACHING LITTLE FINGERS TO PLAY

JOHN THOMPSON'S MODERN COURSE
FOR THE PIANO

TEACHING LITTLE FINGERS
TO PLAY

A BOOK FOR THE EARLIEST
BEGINNER
COMBINING ROTE & NOTE APPROACH
"SOMETHING NEW IN EVERY LESSON"

THE WILLIS MUSIC COMPANY
FLORENCE, KENTUCKY 41042

W.M. Co. 5639

TEACHING LITTLE FINGERS TO PLAY

A method for the early beginner combining rote and note approach. The melodies are written with careful thought and are kept as simple as possible, yet they are refreshingly delightful. All the music lies within the grasp of the child's small hands.

00412076 Book only	$4.95
00406523 Book/CD	$14.95

Foreign Language Editions

00414478 Book only (Spanish Edition)	$3.95
00414498 Book only (French Edition)	$4.50
00416444 Book only (Chinese Edition)	$5.95

SUPPLEMENTARY SERIES
All books include optional teacher accompaniments.

CHRISTMAS FAVORITES
arr. Eric Baumgartner
EARLY ELEMENTARY LEVEL
9 songs celebrating the season: Blue Christmas • The Chipmunk Song • Do You Hear What I Hear • I Heard the Bells on Christmas Day • I'll Be Home for Christmas • The Most Wonderful Time of the Year • Rockin' Around the Christmas Tree • Rudolph the Red-Nosed Reindeer • Silver Bells.

00416721 Book only	$6.95
00416722 Book/CD	$15.95

CLASSICS
arr. Randall Hartsell
EARLY ELEMENTARY LEVEL
11 solos: Barcarolle (Offenbach) • Bridal Chorus (Wagner) • Can-Can (Offenbach) • Country Gardens (English Folk Tune) • A Little Night Music (Mozart) • Lullaby (Brahms) • Ode to Joy (Beethoven) • "Surprise" Symphony (Haydn) • Swan Lake (Tchaikovsky) • Symphony No. 5 (Tchaikovsky) • Turkish March (Beethoven).

00406550 Book only	$5.95
00406736 Book/CD	$15.95

FAMILIAR TUNES
arr. Glenda Austin
EARLY ELEMENTARY LEVEL
17 solos, including: Bingo • Buffalo Gals • If You're Happy and You Know It • I'm a Little Teapot • It's Raining, It's Pouring • Lightly Row • On Top of Old Smoky • Polly Put the Kettle On • Take Me Out to the Ball Game.

00406457 Book only	$5.95
00406740 Book/CD	$15.95

HYMNS
arr. Mary K. Sallee
EARLY ELEMENTARY LEVEL
11 hymns: Amazing Grace • Faith of Our Fathers • For the Beauty of the Earth • Holy, Holy, Holy • Jesus Loves Me • Jesus Loves the Little Children • Joyful, Joyful, We Adore Thee • Kum Bah Yah • Praise Him, All Ye Little Children • We Are Climbing Jacob's Ladder • What a Friend We Have in Jesus.

00406413 Book only	$5.95
00406731 Book/CD	$15.95

JEWISH FAVORITES
arr. Eric Baumgartner
MID-ELEMENTARY LEVEL
9 Klezmer, Israeli, and holiday favorites, including: Heyveynu Shalom Aleichem • Oh Hanukkah • Tumbalalaika • Dayénu • I Have a Little Dreydl • David Melech Yisraél • Nigun • S'vivon • Hatikvah.

00416532 Book only	$5.95
00416670 Book/CD	$15.95

SONGS FROM MANY LANDS
arr. Carolyn C. Setliff
EARLY ELEMENTARY LEVEL
10 piano solos: Beautiful Dreamer • The Blue Bells of Scotland • Cielito Lindo • Du, Du, Liegst Mir im Herzen • Jasmine Flower • Little White Dove • 'O Sole Mio • On the Shore Across the Lake • Song of the Seasons • Sur le Pont d'Avignon.

00416682 Book only	$5.95
00416683 Book/CD	$15.95

*CDs and MIDI disks may be
purchased separately for several titles.*

Also available:

AMERICAN TUNES
arr. Eric Baumgartner
EARLY ELEMENTARY LEVEL

00406753 Book only	$5.95
00406792 Book/CD	$15.90

DISNEY TUNES
arr. Glenda Austin
EARLY ELEMENTARY LEVEL

00416748 Book only	$6.95
00416749 Book/CD	$15.95

BLUES AND BOOGIE
Carolyn Miller
EARLY ELEMENTARY LEVEL

00406539 Book only	$5.95
00406727 Book/CD	$15.95

JAZZ AND ROCK
Eric Baumgartner
EARLY ELEMENTARY LEVEL

00406572 Book only	$5.95
00406718 Book/CD	$15.95

CHRISTMAS CAROLS
arr. Carolyn Miller
EARLY ELEMENTARY LEVEL

00406391 Book only	$6.95
00406722 Book/CD	$15.95

RECITAL PIECES
Carolyn Miller
MID-ELEMENTARY LEVEL

00416539 Book only	$5.95
00416672 Book/CD	$15.95

WILLIS MUSIC

EXCLUSIVELY DISTRIBUTED BY
HAL•LEONARD®
CORPORATION
7777 W. BLUEMOUND RD. P.O. BOX 13819
MILWAUKEE, WISCONSIN 53213

Complete song lists online at **www.halleonard.com**

Prices, contents, and availability subject to change without notice.